ARNE & CARLOS

Knit-and-Crochet

Garden

Bring a Little Outside In: 36 Projects Inspired
by Flowers, Butterflies, Birds and Bees

SEARCH PRESS

Yarn Distributors

For many of the patterns in this book, any yarn can be used; for others, the authors have used a specific yarn or yarns. If you are unable to obtain any of these yarns, you can simply replace them with those of a similar weight and composition.

The distributors that provided all of the yarns for this book are:
Dalegarn: www.dalegarn.com
Rauma Ullvarefabrikk: www.raumaull.no
Sandnes Garn: www.sandnesgarn.no
Bjarne Hjelmtvedt Sytilbehør (Sewing Notions): www.hjelmtvedt.no
Permin: www.permin.dk/no

First published in Great Britain in 2014 by

Search Press Limited, Wellwood, North Farm Road, Tunbridge Wells, Kent TN2 3DR

Also published in the United States of America in 2014 by
Trafalgar Square Books
North Pomfret, Vermont 05053

Originally published in Norwegian as *Håndarbeid fra hagen* by Cappelen Damm A/S

© CAPPELEN DAMM AS 2013
English translation © 2014 Trafalgar Square Books

ISBN 978-1-78221-047-4

Translation: Carol Huebscher Rhoades
Illustrations: Arne & Carlos
Photography: Ragnar Hartvig
Stylist: Ingrid Skansaar
Assistant: Petter Nerjordet
Book Design: Hanne Marie Kjus

Printed in China

10 9 8 7 6 5 4 3 2 1

Publisher's Note:
All of the crochet terms used in this book are standard U.K. terminology.

CONTENTS

FOREWORD

Our garden lies 745 yd / 682 m above the lake, in the Norwegian fells, and is inspired both by the traditional "English Cottage Garden" and cloister gardens with high walls. It is a refuge where we can wander and dream.

Every spring a miracle occurs. First lilies, crocuses, and primroses shoot out their leaves and flowers. Everything happens quickly and soon Veronica and poppies appear and light up the meadow with their blue flowers like a play of sky and water.

Trees, flowers, and bushes screen out passersby and form a protection from the world outside. Small red brick walkways that gleam red after a rain shower help keep the weeds at bay. The stones warm in the sun and give life to the plants in unusual places. The plants also shelter each other. The strong ones protect the weak and less hardy. Within a short time the days lengthen and take over the night, but that doesn't matter. We can sleep when winter comes.

Our garden is prolific with many different spaces: places attuned to various times of the day or year. There are places for sun and places for shade. Open spots and sheltered corners. Hiding places and bathing places. The garden is an extension of the house, a part of the interior with sculpted hedges to provide high walls in the green space and inspire us.

And we are often inspired by the garden. If we are stumped for ideas, nothing works better for generating ideas than digging in the earth. Flowers and plants, colors and shapes— nothing can measure up to nature's design!

We want to welcome you into our little world. You can see a little of the garden and some of the projects we made with inspiration from it. Some of the projects are small and take no time at all to make. The larger projects can take a long time to complete but they don't have to be done quickly, when finished they will make the house and garden more pleasant. If it is something you take pleasure in, then there is time. The larger pieces are comforting projects you can make when it rains and is cold out or if you only want to sit still and let your thoughts fly while your hands work.

We created our garden based on the English model. The garden is a refuge where we can sit and dream and the bench is our favorite place for sitting and crocheting or knitting.

INTRODUCTION

When we first came to the train station that is now our home, there was no garden. The entire yard was a gray platform consisting of tightly packed gray gravel. We soon discovered that we wouldn't simply be able to push a spade into the ground and dig up the soil because there wasn't any soil to dig. That's how a project started that ran parallel with everything else we were working towards: building our own garden.

One who plants a garden, plants happiness

We actually built the garden on top of the platform. We carried huge stones, earth, and bricks by hand to make layers for the flower beds and walkways. We began a long way from the house and worked towards it, and that was a fortunate choice! If we had started near the house and worked out, the garden would have been much smaller. We can say that now; when we started the project we didn't know what we had gotten ourselves into. But no matter how much work there is to do, and how many jobs we have before us, the garden has given us a great deal of satisfaction.

We never imagined the garden would become one of our biggest sources of inspiration. In the beginning, we thought of it more as a cozy place to have during the summer. However, this is what happened: with the flowers and hedges in place, myriads of life came into the previously sad and empty platform. Frogs, bees, butterflies, and other insects, which we hadn't seen there before, popped up and a gray and sad platform was transformed into a delightful and prolific paradise that continually called to us.

And then inspiration came in.

We became fascinated by the insects and butterflies, some of which had accompanied us since the garden was created. We have used butterflies and bees as inspiration for knitting patterns for a very long time and the magnificent colors in the garden inspired us to many new color combinations.

All the patterns in this book are connected to our garden: Each of the projects was directly inspired by it and the flowers or insects described here are now items to use outside, on the terrace, and in other outdoor places.

We were able to take the photographs for the book and use our own garden as the backdrop.

Arne cuts out paper butterflies.

Today Carlos is looking for a spot to take pictures and is using the wheelbarrow to cart around the many heavy blankets.

MATERIALS

The leftover yarn basket is almost empty: Hippie crochets and knits flowers and stripes in every possible color, and it appears that she has cleaned up and made some order in her life. She needs that occasionally. The leftover yarns have become throws, as colorful as her garden and as colorful as she would like the world to be.

In this chapter, we'll try to give detailed information about the materials we used. You'll find a list of yarn sources at the beginning of the book (copyright page): Contact the companies to find out about the shop nearest you.

Yarn

For many of the patterns in this book, we recommend that you use yarn that you've had lying around. Granny squares, garter stitch, and flower throws have been our clearing out projects where we use leftover yarns that we had stashed. For that reason, it is not always possible for us to give you the precise yarn brand or the exact number of balls you need. For other projects, such as the embroidered pillows, Magnus Garden Mouse, clothes for him and Hippie, as well as the knitted bags, we can be more exact: you'll find the information you need with the individual patterns.

Just think ... with a throw you can use up piles of yarn, and it is the randomly chosen colors that make the coverlet charming. So don't try to coordinate the colors too much, just let them be as they are: that way, you'll get the most beautiful result!

Knitting Needles, Crochet Hooks, and Other Needles

You will need double pointed needles (dpn) U.K. sizes 13, 11, and 9–10 / 2.5, 3, and 3.5 mm. You will also need long, straight needles U.K. size 11 / 3 mm for the place mats and kitchen towel with primroses (pages 58-61). 12 in / 33 cm is a suitable length but you can also use a circular needle.

For the potholders, you'll need knitting needles U.K. size 6 / 5 mm. The crochet hook sizes include U.K. sizes 2½ (steel hook), 12, 11, 9, and 6 / 1.5, 2.5, 3, 3.5, and 5 mm. In addition, you'll need a tapestry needle and a blunt tip embroidery needle for embroidering the large pillows.

We pick out an assortment of colors from the leftover yarn basket when we crochet granny squares.

Hippie has cleaned up the sewing room and is ready to start on some projects inspired by our garden.

We are lucky to have a veranda with a roof so we can move the sewing room outside during the summer.

Stuffing

As usual, we have stuffed Magnus Garden Mouse and the Hippies with wool fill (wadding). The fill from Dale Yarn is called Ulltops (wool tops) and Rauma supplies Ullflor (wool carded batts). You will also need something to fill the pillows. We used ready-made pillow forms measuring 24 x 24 in / 60 x 60 cm. You can buy pillow forms at a craft shop or interior furnishing supplier.

Fabric for Pillow Backing

We used a plain weave fabric for the back of the pillows shown on page 70. Basque linen is a good choice and is easy to cut straight. In order to follow the thread lines, just pull out a strand and then you'll have a straight line to cut along.

Buttons

Maybe you are like us and have lots of buttons on hand. If you don't, you'll find a good selection at Bjarne Hjelmtvedt (www. hjelmtvedt.no) or any craft store.

Embroidery Canvas

We used canvas from Permin called "Maxi Canvas" (item #387). You'll find their materials in craft stores and yarn shops, and on-line.

Wind Chimes in the Garden

To make wind chimes, you'll need a good drill, metal rings or nylon cord, and a metal bore for the cord or rings. You can find all of these items at a hardware store. In addition, you'll need some metal chimes such as old silverware or keys.

> NB: Standard U.K. crochet terms are used throughout this book.

Abbreviations

beg	begin, beginning
BO	bind off or cast off (bind off knitwise unless otherwise instructed)
ch	chain (crochet)
cm	centimeter(s)
CO	cast on
dc	double crochet
dpn	double-pointed needle(s)
dtr	double treble crochet
g	gram(s)
k	knit
k2tog	knit 2 together
in	inch(es)
inc	increase with lifted stitches from row below
mm	millimeter(s)
ndl(s)	needle(s)
oz	ounce(s)
p	purl
psso	pass slipped stitch over
rem	remain, remaining
rep	repeat
rnd(s)	round(s)
RS	right side
sl	slip
st(s)	stitch(es)
tbl	through back loop(s)
tr	treble crochet
WS	wrong side
yd	yard(s)
yo	yarnover

Increasing

Increase at the beginning of the row by picking up a stitch at the right side of the stitch below the second stitch on the needle.

Increase at the end of the needle by picking up a stitch on the right side of the stitch below the last stitch on the needle.

All increases for knitted items in this book are made by lifted increases from the stitch below rather than make 1, unless otherwise specified.

MAGNUS
GARDEN MOUSE

We like to decorate the garden. Many years ago, we set out a flower pot filled with pretty, colorful marbles in one of the beds at the side of the Bergenia (elephant-eared saxifrage) that grew bigger and bigger. Finally, the elephant ear leaves grew so big that the pot disappeared under the plant and was forgotten. One day, after many years had passed, we found the pot, but the marbles were gone! We couldn't figure out where they could be or who had taken them, but we knew for sure that neither of us had cleared them away. So, one day, when we wanted to renew a flower bed and lay in some new stones, we found the marbles! It was the garden mouse that had taken them and gathered them in a secret place.

All gardens have one or more mice: Here is the pattern for your own Garden Mouse.

Pattern for Magnus Mouse

MATERIALS

Yarn: One 50 g ball of each color.
Dale of Norway Falk or any other Light DK yarn appropriate for recommended needles.
Light Gray 0004 for the head and body.
Light Pink 4203 for the inside of the ears and nose.
Black 0090 for the eyes.

Needles: Set of 5 dpn U.K. size 13 / 2.5 mm.

INSTRUCTIONS
Begin with the Left Foot

With dpn U.K. size 13 / 2.5 mm, CO 6 sts and divide evenly over 3 dpn, 2 sts on each needle. Join, being careful not to twist cast-on row.
Rnd 1: K6.
Rnd 2: (K1, inc 1, k1) around.
Rnd 3: K9.
Rnd 4: (K1, inc 1, k1, inc 1, k1) around.
Rnd 5: K15.
Rnd 6: (K1, inc 1, k3, inc 1, k1) around – 21 sts.
Knit 9 rnds without increasing.

Sew the tip together,
pull the tail inside the foot and bring it up to use as a marking thread.

Heel and Leg

Work back and forth only over the sts on the first dpn.
Row 1: K7.
Row 2: P7.
Row 3: K7.
Row 4: P7.
Row 5: K7.
Row 6: P7.
Row 7: K7. Using a second dpn, pick up and knit 4 sts on the side of the heel and k7 from dpn. K7 across 3rd dpn; with another dpn, pick up and knit 4 sts along side of heel. Move marking thread so it is between the 1st and 4th dpn.
Now work in the round in stocking stitch, shaping leg as follows:
Rnd 7: Divide the sts onto 4 dpn as you knit around:

Ndl 1: K7.

Ndl 2: K8.

Ndl 3: K6.

Ndl 4: K8.

Rnd 8: Ndl 1: K7.

Ndl 2: K2tog, k6.

Ndl 3: K6.

Ndl 4: K6, k2tog.

Rnd 9: Knit around.

Rnd 10: Ndl 1: K7.

Ndl 2: K2tog, k5.

Ndl 3: K6.

Ndl 4: K5, k2tog.

Rnd 11: Knit around.

Rnd 12: Ndl 1: K2tog, k3, k2tog.

Ndl 2: K2tog, k4.

Ndl 3: K2, k2tog, k2.

Ndl 4: K4, k2tog.

Rnd 13: Knit around – 20 sts rem.

Rnd 14: (K1, k2tog, k2) around.

Rnd 15: Knit.

Rnd 16: (K1, k2tog, k1) around –
12 sts rem.

Fill the foot and leg with wool wadding. Continue in stocking stitch, dividing the sts onto 3 dpn with 4 sts on each needle.

Rnds 17 – 46: K12 (total of 30 rnds).

Rnd 47: K1, inc 1, k10, inc 1, k1.

Rnd 48: Knit.

Rnd 49: K1, inc 1, k12, inc 1, k1.

Rnd 50: Knit.

Rnd 51: BO 2 sts knitwise, k12 including last st from bind-off; BO 2 knitwise. Divide the leg sts onto 2 dpn with 6 sts on each needle. Fill leg with wool wadding.

Right Leg

Work as for the left leg through Rnd 46.

Rnd 47: K5, inc 1, k2, inc 1, k5.

Rnd 48: Knit.

Rnd 49: K6, inc 1, k2, inc 1, k6 – 16 sts.

Rnd 50: Knit.

Rnd 51: K6, BO 4 sts knitwise, k6, including last st from bind-off.

Divide the leg sts onto 2 dpn with 6 sts on each needle. Fill leg with wool wadding.

Join the Legs and Knit the Body

Rnd 1: Begin where the yarn is hanging at the right leg;

Ndl 1:K6 from right leg.

Ndls 2-3: K6 sts each needle from left leg.

Ndl 4: K6 from right leg

Move marker up the side.

The 4 bound-off sts on each leg should be facing each other between the legs.

Rnd 2: K13, inc 1, k10, inc 1, k1.

Rnd 3: K26.

Rnd 4: K13, inc 1, k12, inc 1, k1.

Rnd 5: K28.

Rnd 6: K13, inc 1, k14, inc 1, k1.
Rnd 7: K30.
Rnd 8: K13, inc 1, k16, inc 1, k1.
Rnd 9: K32.
Seam the crotch.
Rnd 10: K13, inc 1, k18, inc 1, k1.
Rnd 11: K34.
Rnd 12: K13, inc 1, k20, inc 1, k1.
Rnd 13: K36.
Rnd 14: K13, inc 1, k22, inc 1, k1.
Rnd 15: K38.
Rnd 16: K13, ssk, k7, k2tog, k2, ssk, k7, k2tog, k1.
Rnd 17: K34.
Rnd 18: K13, ssk, k5, k2tog, k2, ssk, k5, k2tog, k1.
Rnd 19: K30.
Rnd 20: K13, ssk, k3, k2tog, k2, ssk, k3, k2tog, k1.
Rnd 21: K26.
Rnd 22: K13, ssk, k8, k2tog, k1.
Rnd 23: K24.
Rnd 24: BO 2 knitwise, k8, including last st from bind-off, BO 4 knitwise, k8, including last st from bind-off, BO 2 knitwise.

Place the sts for back on one dpn and the sts for front on another dpn.

Arms

With dpn U.K. size 13 / 2.5 mm, CO 6 sts. Divide sts onto 3 dpn and join to work in the round.
Rnd 1: K6.
Rnd 2: (K1, inc 1, k1) around.
Rnd 3: K9.
Rnd 4: (K1, inc 1, k1, inc 1, k1) around.
Rnd 5: K15.
Rnd 6: (K1, inc 1, k3, inc 1, k1) around.

Secure yarn tail at tip of hand and use the tail as a marker.
Rnds 7 – 13: K21.
Rnd 14: (K1, k2tog, k1, k2tog, k1) around.
Rnd 15: K15.
Rnd 16: (K1, k2tog, k2) around.
Rnd 17: K12.
Rnd 18: (K1, k2tog, k1) around.
Fill the hand with wool. Fill the arm with wool wadding every now and then as you work up the arm.
Rnds 19 – 40: K9 (total of 22 rnds).
Rnd 41: BO 2 knitwise, k5 (including last st of bind-off), BO 2 knitwise.
Put the sts from the arm on a holder and make another arm the same way.

Join the body and arms

Rnd 1: Divide the sts onto 4 dpn as follows:
> Back: K8.
> Left arm: K5.
> Front: K8.
> Right arm: K5.

Rnd 2: Back: K1, k2tog, k2, k2tog, k1.
> Left arm: K5.
> Front: K1, k2tog, k2, k2tog, k1.
> Right arm: K5.

Rnd 3: Knit.
Rnd 4: Back: K2, k2tog, k2.
> Left arm: K5.
> Front: K2, k2tog, k2.
> Right arm: K5.

Rnd 5: Knit.
Rnd 6: (K1, k2tog, k2) around.
Rnd 7: Knit.
Rnd 8: (K1, k2tog, k1) around.
Seam the underarms and fill the arms and body with wool wadding.
Rnds 9 – 12: Knit.

Begin Head

Rnd 13: (K1, inc 1, k1, inc 1, k1) around.
Rnd 14: K20.
Rnd 15: (K1, inc 1, k3, inc 1, k1) around.
Rnd 16: K28.
Rnd 17: (K1, inc 1, k5, inc 1 k1) around.
Rnd 18: K36.

Make the hole for the snout

Place the sts on dpn 3 on a waste yarn holder while you work the next 9 rows over dpn 1, 2, and 4.
Row 19: Knit across ndls 1 and 2.
Row 20: Purl across ndls 2, 1, and 4.
Row 21: Knit across ndls 4, 1, and 2.
Row 22: Purl across ndls 2, 1, and 4.
Row 23: Knit across ndls 4, 1, and 2.
Row 24: Purl across ndls 2, 1, and 4.
Row 25: Knit across ndls 4, 1, and 2.
Row 26: Purl across ndls 2, 1, and 4.
Row 27: Knit across ndls 4, 1, and 2.
CO 9 sts onto a new dpn, over the ones on a holder from dpn 3. Knit around all 4 dpn. The hole for the snout is now complete. Continue working in the round over all 4 dpn.
Rnd 28: K36.
Rnd 29: (K1, k2tog, k3, k2tog, k1) around.
Rnd 30: K28.
Rnd 31: (K1, k2tog, k1, k2tog, k1) around.
Rnd 32: K20.
Rnd 33: (K1, k2tog, k2) around.
Rnd 34: K16.
Rnd 35: (K1, k2tog, k1) around.
Rnd 36: K12.
Cut yarn and draw through remaining 12 sts.
Seam the hole and weave in end on WS.

Make the snout

Pick up and knit 9 sts on each of the sides and over the hole for the snout; divide the sts over 4 dpn.
Rnds 1 – 3: K36.
Rnd 4: (K1, k2tog, k3, k2tog, k1) around.
Rnds 5 – 7: K28.
Rnd 8: (K1, k2tog, k1, k2tog, k1) around.
Rnds 9 – 11: K20.
Rnd 12: (K1, k2tog, k2) around.
Rnds 13 – 15: K16.
Rnd 16: (K1, k2tog, k1) around.
Change to pink 4203.
Rnds 17 – 19: K12.
Cut yarn and draw through remaining 12 sts.
Fill with wool and seam the hole on the snout.
Weave in ends.

Magnus has found a hiding place in the garden. Do you think he has our marbles there?

Ears for the Garden Mouse

Make 2 triangles with gray and 2 triangles with pink as follows:
With ndls U.K. size 13 / 2.5 mm, CO 10 sts.
Row 1: Purl.

Row 2: Knit.
Row 3: Purl.
Row 4: Knit.
Row 5: Purl.
Row 6: K1, k2tog, k4, k2tog, k1.
Row 7: Purl.
Row 8: Knit.
Row 9: Purl.
Row 10: K1, k2tog, k2, k2tog, k1.
Row 11: Purl.
Row 12: K1, k2tog, k2tog, k1.
Row 13: P4.
Row 14: K1, k2tog, k1.
BO purlwise.
Place a pink triangle with WS facing WS against a gray triangle and crochet them together with dc on the long sides, using gray yarn on the pink side.

Crochet the other ear together the same way. Use your index finger to curve each ear and sew ears to the head.

Tail
With 2 dpn U.K. size 13 / 2.5 mm, CO 4 sts; join to work in the round. Work around in stocking stitch until tail is desired length – the tail on our mouse is 8 in / 20 cm long.

BO and sew the tail to the center back of the body, about ⅝ in / 1.5 cm from the crotch seam. Weave in the yarn tail at the end of the mouse tail.

Sweaters for Magnus

Five sweaters are knit with leftover yarns. One sweater takes so little yarn that it doesn't even register on the kitchen scale. We've written the pattern for a striped sweater but you can also make it in a single color.

Magnus Garden Mouse doesn't have a mouth and he can be so sweet without one. He only has two diamond-shaped eyes that squint in the sun.

MATERIALS
Yarn: Small amounts of Dale of Norway Falk, Rauma Finullgarn, Sandnes Smart or any other yarn appropriate for recommended needles. You have lots of colors to choose from with these yarns.

Needles: set of 5 dpn U.K. sizes 11 and 9–10 / 3 and 3.5 mm.

INSTRUCTIONS

Body

With smaller size dpn, CO 40 sts and divide evenly onto dpn (10 sts on each needle). Join, being careful not to twist cast-on row.

Rnds 1 – 7: Work in k2, p2 ribbing. Change to larger dpn and continue in stripe pattern:

Rnds 8 – 13: Knit, changing colors every two rnds.

Rnd 14: Work with the same color as the ribbing. BO 2 knitwise, k16 (including the last st from bind-off), BO 4 knitwise, k16 (including last st from bind-off), BO 2 knitwise.
Divide the sts for front and back onto 2 dpn with 16 sts on each needle.

Sleeves

With smaller dpn, CO 16 sts and divide evenly onto 4 dpn (4 sts on each needle).

Rnds 1 – 4: Work in k2, p2 ribbing. Change to larger dpn and continue in stripe pattern:

Rnds 5 – 14: Knit, changing colors every two rnds.

Rnd 15: BO 2 knitwise, k12 (including last st from bind-off), BO 2 knitwise.
Place sts on a holder and make the other sleeve the same way.

Join Body and Sleeves

Divide the 56 sts onto 4 dpn as follows:

Rnd 1: Back: K16.
        Left sleeve: K12.
        Front: K16.
        Right sleeve: K12.

Rnd 2: Work (K1, k2tog, k10, k2tog, k13) 2 times – 4 sts decreased, 52 sts rem.

Rnd 3: Knit.

Rnd 4: Work (K1, k2tog, k8, k2tog, k13) 2 times – 48 sts rem.

Rnd 5: Knit.

Rnd 6: Work (K1, k2tog, k6, k2tog, k1) around – 8 sts decreased, 40 sts rem.

Rnd 7: Knit.

Rnd 8: Work (K1, k2tog, k4, k2tog, k1) around – 32 sts rem.

Rnd 9: Knit.

Divide the remaining 32 sts onto 4 smaller size dpn (8 sts on each needle) and finish with 6 rnds of k2, p2 ribbing.
BO.
Seam the underarms and weave in all ends neatly on WS.
Gently steam press the sweater on the stocking stitch areas (do not press the ribbing).

Pants for Magnus

MATERIALS

Yarn: Small amounts of Dale of Norway Falk, Rauma Finullgarn, Sandnes Smart or any other yarn appropriate for recommended needles. You have lots of colors to choose from with these yarns.

Needles: set of 5 dpn U.K. sizes 11 and 9–10 / 3 and 3.5 mm.
Crochet hook: U.K. size 11 / 3 mm

INSTUCTIONS

Legs

With smaller dpn, CO 24 sts and divide evenly onto 4 dpn (6 sts on each needle). Join, being careful not to twist cast-on row. Begin with garter st in the round:
Rnd 1: Purl.

Rnd 2: Knit.
Rnd 3: Purl.
Rnd 4: Knit.
Rnd 5: Purl.
Change to larger dpn and knit 20 rnds.
Rnd 26: BO 3 knitwise, k18 (including last st of bind-off), BO 3 knitwise.
Divide sts onto 2 dpn with 9 sts on each. Make the other leg the same way.

Join both legs

Beginning at the front with the left leg, divide sts onto 4 dpn.
Rnds 27 – 31: K36.
Rnd 32: K16, BO 4 knitwise, k16 (including last st of bind-off).
Rnd 33: K16, CO 4 new sts over the bound-off sts, k16.
Rnds 34 – 35: K36.
Change to smaller dpn and work 7 rnds in k2, p2 ribbing.
BO; sew crotch seam. With crochet hook, work dc around the hole for the tail.

Weave in all ends neatly on WS. Gently steam press the pants on the stocking stitch areas (do not press the ribbing).

Overalls for Magnus

MATERIALS

Yarn: Small amounts of Dale of Norway Falk, Rauma Finullgarn, Sandnes Smart or any other yarn appropriate for recommended needles. You have lots of colors to choose from with these yarns.

Needles: set of 5 dpn U.K. sizes 11 and 9–10 / 3 and 3.5 mm.
Crochet hook: U.K. size 11 / 3 mm

Follow the instructions for the pants through Rnd 35.
Rnd 36: Divide the sts onto 4 dpn as follows:
  Ndl 1: K6 with larger size dpn.
  Ndl 2: Change to smaller dpn and p2tog, p1, k2, p2tog, p1, k2, p2tog.
  Ndl 3: P2tog, k2, p2tog, p1, k2, p2tog, p1.
  Ndl 4: Change to larger dpn and k6.

Knit the sts on ndl 1 once more.
Move marker so it is after ndl 1.
Sts on ndls 1 and 4 form the bib on the pants.
Rnds 37 – 43: Work 12 sts in stocking stitch with larger size dpn on ndls 1 and 4 and work 18 sts in p2, k2 ribbing with smaller needles on ndls 2 and 3. Finish with p2 on ndl 3.
Rnd 44: BO 2 purlwise and BO 2 knitwise, k4 (including last st of bind-off = strap), BO 2 purlwise, k4 (including last st of bind-off = strap), BO 2 knitwise and BO 2 purlwise. Knit the remaining 12 sts on larger needle. Place the strap sts on separate waste yarn holders. Finish the bib with 10 rows in stocking stitch worked back and forth on larger needles. BO knitwise.

Straps
Place the strap sts on separate, smaller size needles for each (= 4 sts on each needle) and work each strap separately as follows: Work 19 rows back and forth in stocking stitch. BO purlwise.

Neckband around the Bib and Straps
Beginning on left side, work dc around the edge. At each of the 2 corners of the bib and lower edge of the straps, work 3 dc. At the tip of each strap, crochet button loops: *3 dc in 1st corner, 2 dc along the end and 2 dc in the 2nd corner, turn and ch 4, 1 sl st in the 1st corner, 6 dc in the chain-loop and 1 dc in the 2nd corner*. Work around the tail opening in dc.

Weave in ends on WS and gently steam press overalls; sew on buttons.

Garden Tips! If you plant tightly spaced, the plants will give each other protection and support. They help each other to grow and help keep the weeds away. When the plants become too tightly packed, you can share any extras with friends.

THE HIPPIES

A flower garden has to have flower children. At this very moment, two have arrived in their VW bus. Hippies don't like to live alone so it won't be long before there are more. Some come because they are invited, others just show up—that's how hippies are.

Knit a Hippie

Little flower children knitted with leftover yarns.

MATERIALS

Yarn: One 50 g ball color 3102 for skin. Dale of Norway Falk or any other Light DK yarn appropriate for recommended needles.
Use leftover yarns for the top of the body and the legs.

White 0020.
Beige 2642.
Brown 3072.
Dark brown 2671.
Black 0090
Note: These color numbers might change and new colors might be added to the selection with different color numbers.

Needles: Set of 5 dpn U.K. size 13 / 2.5 mm.

INSTRUCTIONS

Begin with the Left Foot

With dpn U.K. size 13 / 2.5 mm, CO 6 sts and divide evenly over 3 dpn, 2 sts on each needle. Join, being careful not to twist cast-on row.
Rnd 1: K6.
Rnd 2: (K1, inc 1, k1) around.
Rnd 3: K9.
Rnd 4: (K1, inc 1, k1, inc 1, k1) around.
Rnd 5: K15.
Rnd 6: (K1, inc 1, k3, inc 1, k1) around – 21 sts.
Knit 9 rnds without increasing.

Sew the tip together, pull the tail inside the foot, bring it up and use it as a marking thread.

Heel and Leg

Work back and forth only over the sts on the first dpn.
Row 1: K7.
Row 2: P7.
Row 3: K7.
Row 4: P7.
Row 5: K7.
Row 6: P7.
Row 7: K7. Using a second dpn, pick up and knit 4 sts on the side of the heel and k7 from dpn. K7 across 3rd dpn; with another dpn, pick up and knit 4 sts along side of heel. Move marking thread so it is between the 1st and 4th dpn.

Now work in the round in stocking stitch, shaping leg as follows:

Rnd 7: Divide the sts onto 4 dpn as you knit around:

> Ndl 1: k7.
> Ndl 2: K8.
> Ndl 3: K6.
> Ndl 4: K8.

Rnd 8: Ndl 1: K7.

> Ndl 2: K2tog, k6.
> Ndl 3: K6.
> Ndl 4: K6, k2tog.

Rnd 9: Knit around.

Rnd 10: Ndl 1: K7.

> Ndl 2: K2tog, k5.
> Ndl 3: K6.
> Ndl 4: K5, k2tog.

Rnd 11: Knit around.

Rnd 12: Ndl 1: K2tog, k3, k2tog.

> Ndl 2: K2tog, k4.
> Ndl 3: K2, k2tog, k2.
> Ndl 4: K4, k2tog.

Rnd 13: Knit around.

Rnd 14: (K1, k2tog, k2) around.

Rnd 15: Knit.

Rnd 16: (K1, k2tog, k1) around.

Fill the foot and leg with wool wadding. Continue in stocking stitch, dividing the sts onto 3 dpn with 4 sts on each needle.

Rnds 17 – 46: K12 (total of 30 rnds).

Rnd 47: K1, inc 1, k10, inc 1, k1.

Rnd 48: Knit.

Rnd 49: K1, inc 1, k12, inc 1, k1.

Rnd 50: Knit.

Rnd 51: BO 2 sts knitwise, k12 including last st from bind-off; BO 2 knitwise. Divide the leg sts onto 2 dpn with 6 sts on each needle. Fill leg with wool wadding.

Right Leg

Work as for the left leg through Rnd 46.

Rnd 47: K5, inc 1, k2, inc 1, k5.

Rnd 48: Knit.

Rnd 49: K6, inc 1, k2, inc 1, inc 1, k6.

Rnd 50: Knit.

Rnd 51: K6, BO 4 sts knitwise, k6, including last st from bind-off. Divide the leg sts onto 2 dpn with 6 sts on each needle. Fill leg with wool wadding.

Join the Legs and Knit the Body

Rnd 1: Begin where the yarn is hanging at the right leg.

> Ndl 1: K6 from right leg.
> Ndls 2-3: K6 on each needle from left leg.
> Ndl 4: K6 from right leg

Move marker up the side.

The 4 bound-off sts on each leg should be facing each other between the legs.

Rnds 2 – 6: K24 (5 rnds total).

Change to T-shirt color if you want a difference between the pant legs and the top. Seam the crotch.

Rnds 7 – 23: K24 (17 rnds total).

Rnd 24: BO 2 knitwise, k8 (including last st of bind-off), BO 4 knitwise, k8 (including last st of bind-of), BO 2 knitwise.

Place the sts of front and back on separate needles.

Arms

With skin color and dpn U.K. size 13 / 2.5 mm, CO 6 sts. Divide sts onto 3 dpn and join to work in the round.

Rnd 1: K6.

Rnd 2: (K1, inc 1, k1) around.

Rnd 3: K9.

Rnd 4: (K1, inc 1, k1, inc 1, k1) around.

Rnd 5: K15.

Rnd 6: (K1, inc 1, k3, inc 1, k1) around.

Secure yarn tail at tip of hand and bring up tail to use as a marker.

Rnds 7 – 13: K21.

Rnd 14: (K1, k2tog, k1, k2tog, k1) around.

Rnd 15: K15.

Rnd 16: (K1, k2tog, k2) around.

Rnd 17: K12.

Rnd 18: (K1, k2tog, k1) around.

Fill the hand with wool. Fill the arm with wool every now and then as you work up the arm. If you want a long-sleeve sweater, change colors on the next rnd. If you want a T-shirt, work, for example, 15 rnds with skin color before changing.

Rnds 19 – 40: K9 (total of 22 rnds).

Rnd 41: BO 2 knitwise, k5 (including last st of bind-off), BO 2 knitwise.

Put the sts from the arm on a holder and make another arm the same way.

Join the Body and Arms

Rnd 1: Divide the sts onto 4 dpn as follows:

Back: K8.
Left arm: K5.
Front: K8.
Right arm: K5.

Rnd 2: Back: K1, k2tog, k2, k2tog, k1.
Left arm: K5.
Front: K1, k2tog, k2, k2tog, k1.
Right arm: K5.

Rnd 3: Knit.

Rnd 4: Back: K2, k2tog, k2.
Left arm: K5.
Front: K2, k2tog, k2.
Right arm: K5.

Rnd 5: Knit – 20 sts rem.

Seam the underarms; change to skin color.

Rnd 6: (K1, k2tog, k2) around.

Rnd 7: Knit.

Rnd 8: (K1, k2tog, k1) around – 12 sts rem.

Fill arms and body with wool wadding.

Rnds 9 – 12: Knit.

Begin Head

Rnd 13: (K1, inc 1, k1, inc 1, k1) around.

Rnd 14: K20.

Rnd 15: (K1, inc 1, k3, inc 1, k1) around.

Rnd 16: K28.

Rnd 17: (K1, inc 1, k5, inc 1 k1) around.

Rnd 18: K36.

Rnd 19: (K1, inc 1, k7, inc 1 k1) around.

Rnd 20: K44.

Rnd 21: (K1, inc 1, k9, inc 1 k1) around.

Rnd 22: K52.

Rnd 23: (K1, inc 1, k11, inc 1 k1) around.

Rnds 24 – 26: K60.

Rnd 27: Knit around and place a marker around the 8th st on the 3rd ndl. There should be 3 sts between the eyes when they are embroidered and this st will be at the center.

Rnds 28 – 30: K60.

Rnd 31: (K1, k2tog, k9, k2tog, k1) around.

Rnd 32: K52.

Rnd 33: (K1, k2tog, k7, k2tog, k1) around.

Rnd 34: K44.

Rnd 35: (K1, k2tog, k5, k2tog, k1) around.

Rnd 36: K36.

Rnd 37: (K1, k2tog, k3, k2tog, k1) around.

Rnd 38: K28.

Rnd 39: (K1, k2tog, k1, k2tog, k1) around.

Rnd 40: K20.

Rnd 41: (K1, k2tog, k2) around.

Rnd 42: K16.

Rnd 43: (K1, k2tog, k1) around.

Cut yarn and draw through remaining 12 sts.

Fill head with wool wadding, tighten end through the top sts and weave in ends neatly on WS.

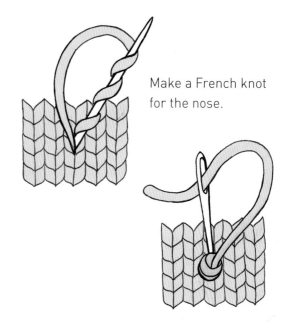

Make a French knot for the nose.

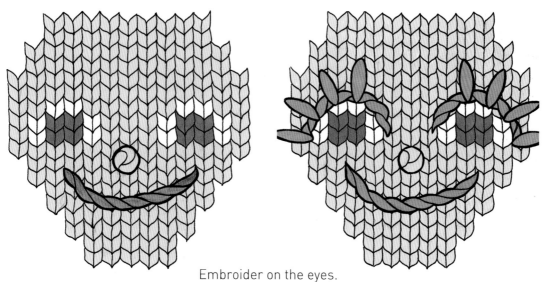

Embroider on the eyes.
Sew on the eyelashes and mouth with back stitch.

Look at My Dress

Our dresses are in every color imaginable. Green, blue, red, white, black and many others. But just listen to what I'm telling you: green, blue, red, white, black, and many others.

Quoted from "Traditional Children's Songs"

MATERIALS

The dresses in the book are knitted with various leftover yarns, but all were worked on needles U.K. size 9–10 / 3.5 mm. They vary a bit in size but that doesn't matter to the Hippie. She likes them both long and short.

Needles: set of 5 U.K. sizes 11 and 9–10 / 3 and 3.5 mm
Crochet Hook: U.K size 11 / 3 mm

INSTRUCTIONS

Dress

With smaller dpn, CO 40 and divide sts evenly onto 4 dpn (10 sts on each needle). Join, being careful not to twist cast-on row.

Garter Stitch and Lace Edging

Rnd 1: P40.
Rnd 2: (K2tog, yo) around – don't forget the last yarnover, at the end of the round.
Rnd 3: P40.
Rnd 4: K40.
Rnd 5: Change to larger needles and k40.
Rnds 6 – 10: K40.

Rnd 11: (K1, k2tog, k4, k2tog, k1) around.
Rnds 12 – 16: K32.
Rnd 17: (K1, k2tog, k2, k2tog, k1) around.
Rnds 18 – 22: K24.

Front Panel

Move the 12 sts for the front from 2 needles onto one needle and work back and forth in stocking stitch.
Row 1: K12.
Row 2: P12.
Row 3: K1, k2tog, k6, k2tog, k1.
Row 4: P10.
Row 5: K10.
Row 6: P10.
BO knitwise.

Back

Move the 12 sts for the back from 2 needles onto one needle and work back and forth in stocking stitch.
Row 1: K12.
Row 2: P12.
Row 3: K1, k2tog, k6, k2tog, k1
Row 4: P10.

Row 5: K10.

Row 6: P10.

Row 7: K4, BO 2 knitwise, k4 (including last st of bind-off). Divide the sts onto 2 dpn (= 4 sts on each needle = straps).

Straps

Work back and forth in stocking stitch. Work each strap separately.

Row 1: P4.

Row 2: K4.

Row 3: P4.

Row 4: K4.

Row 5: P4.

Row 6: K4.

Row 7: P4.

Row 8: K4.

Row 9: P4.

BO knitwise. Weave in ends neatly on WS.

Flower Ruffles to Hem the Dress

Use crochet hook U.K. size 11 / 3 mm.

Rnd 1: Begin with 1 dc in the lace eyelet at center back, (ch 4, 1 dc in the next eyelet) around and end with 1 sl st in the first ch.

Rnd 2: (1 sl st, ch 2, 2 tr, 2 ch and 1 dc) in every ch loop. End with 1 dc in the first ch loop.

Crocheted Edges

Work dc around the armholes and straps. At the end of each strap, make a button loop as follows:

Work *3 dc in 1st corner, 2 dc along the end, and 2 dc in the 2nd corner; turn and ch 4, 1 sl st in the 1st corner, 6 dc in the chain-loop and 1 dc in the 2nd corner*. Weave in all ends neatly on WS. Gently steam press dress. Sew on the "just right" buttons.

Fine!

Flower Shoes

Just like slipping your feet into a flower.

MATERIALS
Yarn: Small amounts of yarn appropriate for recommended needles.

Needles: Set of 5 dpn U.K. size 9–10 / 3.5 mm; **Crochet Hook:** U.K. size 9 / 3.5 mm

INSTRUCTIONS
Begin with the toe. CO 8 sts onto one needle and then divide sts onto 4 dpn with 2 sts on each needle. Join, being careful not to twist cast-on row.
Rnd 1: K8.
Rnd 2: (K1, inc 1, k1) around.
Rnd 3: K12.
Rnd 4: (K1, inc 1, k1, inc 1, k1) around.
Rnd 5: K20.
Rnd 6: (K1, inc 1, k3, inc 1, k1) around – 28 sts.
Sew the toe closed and weave in ends on WS.
Knit 12 rnds (28 sts each rnd).

Heel
Work the heel back and forth in short rows over sts on needles 1 and 2 only.
Row 1: K9, k2tog.
Row 2: P5, p2tog.
Row 3: K5, k2tog.
Row 4: P5, p2tog.
Row 6: P5, p2tog.

Row 7: K5, k2tog.
Row 8: P5, p2tog.
Knit 2 rnds over all the sts, dividing sts over 4 dpn with 5 sts on each needle. Finish with 10 rnds k2, p2 ribbing.

Crocheted Flower Frills
Work crochet from the inside of the ribbing using crochet hook U.K. size 9 / 3.5 mm.
Rnd 1: Begin by inserting the hook between 2 knit sts and work 1 dc. Work (ch 4, 1 dc between 2 purl sts, ch 4, 1 dc between 2 knit sts) around; end with 1 sl st into 1st dc.
Rnd 2: Work (1 dc, ch 2, 2 tr, ch 2, 1 dc) in each ch loop around. End with 1 sl st into 1st dc.
Cut yarn and weave in ends neatly on WS. Gently steam press stocking stitch parts of shoes; do not press ribbing.

Bumblebee Man

Like a bumblebee, this little man flies from flower to flower, creating life and growth in the garden. He is very shy and often pulls his sweater up to his eyes.

This pattern can be used for both a bee and a ladybug.

MATERIALS

Yarn: Dale of Norway Falk
One ball of each color:
Black 0090
Yellow 2417
Light Pink 3102
White 0017
Blue 5545
Red 3609

Needles: set of 5 dpn U.K. size 13 / 2.5 mm

INSTRUCTIONS

Begin with the Left Foot

With black, CO 6 sts; divide over 3 dpn with 2 sts on each needle. Join, being careful not to twist cast-on row.
Rnd 1: K6.
Rnd 2: (K1, inc 1, k1) around.
Rnd 3: K9.
Rnd 4: (K1, inc 1, k1, inc 1, k1) around.
Rnds 5 – 10: K15 (= 6 rnds total).
Use the cast-on tail to sew up the tip of the foot; bring the yarn up and use it as a marking thread.

Heel and Leg

Work back and forth only over the sts on the first needle (5 sts).
Row 1: K5.
Row 2: P5.
Row 3: K5.
Row 4: P5.
Now return to knitting in the round:
Rnd 11: K5; with the 2nd ndl, pick up and knit 3 sts on the side of the heel and then the 5 sts on ndl. K5 on ndl 3 and then, with a new needle, pick up and knit 3 sts on side of heel. Move marker so it is between ndls 1 and 4. Continue working stocking stitch in the round, decreasing as follows:
Rnd 12: Divide sts over 4 needles:
    Ndl 1: K5.
    Ndl 2: K6.
    Ndl 3: K4.
    Ndl 4: K6.
Rnd 13: Ndl 1: K5.
    Ndl 2: K2tog, k4.
    Ndl 3: K4.
    Ndl 4: K4, k2tog.
Rnd 14: K19.
Rnd 15: Ndl 1: K1, k2tog, k2.
    Ndl 2: K1, k2tog, k2.
    Ndl 3: K4.
    Ndl 4: K1, k2tog, k2.

Mini-blanket and mini-pillow

MATERIALS

You'll need a single ply Crewel yarn in an assortment of colors and crochet hook U.K. size
2½ steel / 1.5 mm.

INSTRUCTIONS

Crocheted Mini-Squares

Rnd 1: Ch 6 and join into a ring with 1 sl st into 1st ch.

Rnd 2: Ch 4 (= 1 dtr), 3 dtr around ring, ch 3, (4 dtr around ring, ch 3) 3 times (= 4 dtr groups total). End with 1 sl st into 1st dtr.

Rnd 3: Change color. Turn work and ch 4 (= 1 dtr), 3 dtr around ch loop, ch 3, 4 dtr into same ch loop, ch 2, (4 dtr around next ch loop, ch 3, 4 dtr around same loop, ch 2)

a total of 3 times (= 2 dtr groups in each corner). End with 1 sl st into top of ch 4. Cut yarn and weave in ends.

The finished blanket has 72 small squares sewn together, 9 in length and 8 in width. Sew the squares together with regular sewing thread.

The finished pillow top has 12 small squares sewn together, 3 in width and 4 in length. The squares are sewn together with regular sewing thread. The pillow is sewn with a cotton canvas and filled with wool. The crocheted fabric is sewn onto the finished pillow, with one stitch in each loop and a stitch between each square.

44

The Bird House

This house has three apartments. This year the apartment on the second floor had a view of the lake and was occupied by a pair of flycatchers.

In the spring the garden always has places for the birds and it is clear that they should also have their own space! We have built many birdhouses to place around the garden and they are used every single summer. It is good to see that the guests are so satisfied with the service here that they come back year after year.

TIPS: Build a birdhouse and let children decorate it. That way they will be guaranteed to appreciate it. This birdhouse was painted by Carlos' niece Maddy when she was 5 years old.

Potholders Inspired by the Birdhouse in the Garden

Potholders inspired by the colors on an old pillow found in a junk store in Columbus, Ohio. They serve as decoration on the terrace and, at the same time, are practical if you hang them near the grill.

MATERIALS

Yarn: Dale of Norway Freestyle
For the potholders:
1 ball yellow 2106
1 ball black 0090
For the embroidery (small amounts of each color):
Green 9133
Blue 6015
Dark blue 5626
Purple 4845
Red-orange 3309

Needles: U.K. size 6 / 5 mm, straight ndls
Crochet hook: U.K. size 6 / 5 mm

INSTRUCTIONS
Potholders

Each potholder consists of 2 pieces that are crocheted together with WS facing WS and double crochet in the lace eyelets around the edge.
With knitting needles and yellow, CO 29 and work back and forth in stocking stitch as follows:

Row 1: K29.
Row 2: P29.
Row 3: K2, (yo, k2tog) to last st and end k1.
Row 4: P29.
Row 5: K29.
Row 6: P29.
Row 7: K2, yo, k2tog, k22, yo, k2tog, k1.
Repeat Rows 4 – 7 a total of 8 more times.
Row 40: P29.
Row 41: K1, k2tog, k23, k2tog, k1.
Row 42: P27.
Row 43: K1, k2tog, yo, k2tog, k17, k2tog, yo, k2tog, k1.
Row 44: P25.
Row 45: K1, k2tog, k19, k2tog, k1.
Row 46: P23.
Row 47: K1, k2tog, yo, k2tog, k13, k2tog, yo, k2tog, k1.
Row 48: P21.
Row 49: K1, k2tog, k15, k2tog, k1.
Row 50: P19.
Row 51: K1, k2tog, yo, k2tog, k9, k2tog, yo, k2tog, k1.
Row 52: P17.
Row 53: K1, k2tog, k11, k2tog, k1.

Embroidery

Embroider around the hole for the bird-house with black: Count down 28 sts from the top and to the center st of the row. The center st is also the middle of the 3 sts at the top of the hole.

Sew on the flowers in desired colors and finish with stalks and leaves.

Joining the Pieces

Crochet the front and back of the potholder together with treble crochet in all the lace eyelets along the edge. Begin at one lower corner with 10 tr around the 1st eyelet, 3 tr in each of the next 7 eyelets, turn the corner with 5 tr in the corner eyelet, work 3 tr in each of the next 7 eyelets up to the roof ridge, 6 tr in the eyelet at the roof ridge, ch 5 and work 6 tr in the same eyelet. Continue with 3 tr in each of the next 7 eyelets, turn the corner with 5 tr in the corner eyelet, work 3 tr in each of the next 7 eyelets and 10 tr in the 2nd lower corner. Work 3 tr in each of the next 11 eyelets and join with 1 sl st to 1st tr.

Cut yarn and weave in ends neatly to WS. Gently steam press potholder.

Row 54: P15.
Row 55: K1, k2tog, yo, k2tog, k5, k2tog, yo, k2tog, k1.
Row 56: P13.
Row 57: K1, k2tog, k7, k2tog, k1.
Row 58: P11.
Row 59: K1, k2tog, yo, k2tog, k1, k2tog, yo, k2tog, k1.
Row 60: P9.
Row 61: K1, k2tog, k3, k2tog, k1.
Row 62: P7.
Row 63: K2, yo, sl 1, k2tog, psso, yo, k2.
Row 64: P7.
Row 65: K1, k2tog, k1, k2tog, k1.
Row 66: P5.
Row 67: K2, yo, k2tog, k1.
Row 68: P5.
BO knitwise.

BRAMBLY HEDGE

SPRING STORY

JILL BARKLEM

SPRING FLOWERS

The work in the garden begins long before the snow melts. We sketch out our plans for the coming summer, get out the inspirational books, and check our notes from the previous year. Primroses, auricula (mountain cowslip), and potted plants add a splash of color in early and mid-spring. We have always said that primroses are best used as borders.

Primrose Granny Squares

Primroses are a sure sign of spring. We usually buy potted primroses at Easter time. We keep these inside until summer arrives. Then we take the pots out where they can stay for the entire summer. Finally we plant them in the beds: some of them will survive beneath the cover of snow and come back the next year.

MATERIALS

Yarn: For the flowers: small amounts of yarn to crochet with recommended hook size

For the granny squares:

Dale of Norway Falk: black 0090; one 50g ball will be enough for approx 8 squares (**Note:** illustrations were done in white)

Crochet hook: U.K. size 9 / 3.5 mm

INSTRUCTIONS

Flower

Rnd 1: Ch 8 and join into a ring with 1 sl st into 1st ch.

Rnd 2: Ch 3 (= 1 tr), 15 tr around ring (=16 tr total). End with a sl st into top of ch 3.

Rnd 3: Change color. Work 1 dc between 2 tr, ch 5, (1 dc between the 2nd and 3rd tr from the hook, ch 5) around (= 8 ch loops). End with 1 sl st into 1st dc.

Rnd 4: Change color. (1 dc, ch 3, 4 dtr, ch 3, 1 dc into same ch loop) in each ch loop around. End with 1 sl st into 1st dc.

Background Color

Crochet into the back of the flower in the sts between the flower petals, on the 3rd rnd of the flower. Make sure that the background doesn't show through the flower.

Rnd 1: Work 1 dc, ch 6 (= 1 dtr and 3 ch), 1 dtr in the same st, ch 2, 1 tr in the next st, ch 2, (1 dtr in the next st, ch 3, 1 dtr in the same st, ch 2, 1 tr in next st, ch 2) a total of 3 times (= 4 corners and 4 sides). End with 1 sl st into 1st dtr.

Rnd 2: Ch 4 (= 1 dtr), 2 dtr in ch-3 loop, ch 3, 3 dtr in the same ch loop, (ch 2, 3 dtr in next ch-2 loop) 2 times, ch 2, *3 dtr in ch-3 loop, ch 3, 3 dtr in the same ch loop, (ch 2, 3 dtr in next ch-2 loop) 2 times, ch 2*; rep * to * a total of 3 times. End with 1 sl st into 1st dtr.

Rnd 3: Turn work and crochet back. Ch 4 (= 1 dtr), 2 dtr in ch-2 loop, (ch 2, 3 dtr in next ch-2 loop) 2 times, ch 2, 3 dtr in ch-3 loop, ch 3, 3 dtr in the same ch loop, *(ch 2, 3 dtr in the next ch-2 loop) 3 times, ch 2, 3 dtr in ch-3 loop, ch 3, 3 dtr in the same ch loop*; rep * to * a total of 3 times. End with 1 sl st into 1st dtr. Cut yarn and pull through last st.

Joining the Squares

See page 92 for an illustrated lesson on how to join the squares. Begin by crocheting squares together one by one until you've gone across the width of the blanket. First crochet an edge on the first square or strip:

Begin in one corner and work 1 dc in ch loop, ch 3, 1 dc in same loop, *1 dc between the 1st and 2nd sts in the dtr group, ch 3, 1 dc between the 2nd and 3rd sts in the dtr group, 1 dc in ch loop, ch 3 and 1 dc in the same ch loop*; rep from * to * to the corner and work 1 dc in ch loop, ch 1.

Now join the first square with the second square or strip without cutting the yarn:

Begin in the corner with the second square and work 1 tr in ch loop, ch 3 and 1 dc in the same ch loop. Work 1 tr into the dc at the corner of the first square and then 1 dc in the loop you just crocheted on the second square. Work 1 dc between the 1st and 2nd dtr in the dtr group of the second square, ch 1, 1 dc in the next ch loop of the first square, ch 1, 1 dc between the 2nd and 3rd st in the dtr group of the second square, 1 dc in ch loop of the second square, ch 1, 1 dc in the next ch loop of the first square, ch 1, 1 dc in the same ch loop of the second square*; rep * to * to the corner.

Cut yarn and pull through last st. Now you can crochet the squares together one by one until you reach desired length. The strips are crocheted together the same way but, in the space between the squares, work 1 dc in the tr of one strip, ch 3 and 1 dc in the tr on the second strip.

The flowers made like this are a great way to use up leftover yarns. We used Dale of Norway Falk and Heilo, Rauma Finullgarn, Peer Gynt, Sisu, and some other yarns that we aren't sure about because they've been around so long. The most important thing when choosing the yarns is that they work easily with a U.K. 9 / 3.5 mm hook.

Tips: You can crochet the 1st and 2nd rounds in one color and the 3rd and 4th rounds in another color or use 1 color for Rnds 1 and 2, a second color for Rnd 3, and then a third color for the 4th round. We did a little of everything. We used black for the background color. We have crocheted some larger throws with granny squares but they are almost too big so we usually make somewhat smaller and cozier throws. They should be big enough to throw over yourself while you sit outside, rest on the sofa, or chill a bit on a cold winter day. The squares can also be used for pillows, potholders, or maybe as shown here, for our little puppy Freja's dog blanket.

Freja's Blanket

Crochet the blanket in the size you like. We made a dog blanket 7 flowers high and 7 flowers wide. For the background and joining, you can use Dale of Norway Falk black 0090 or black Smart from Sandnes. It took about 600 g black. Freja's blanket has a total of 49 squares and measures 33½ x 33½ in / 85 x 85 cm.

Edging on Freja's Blanket
Work 2 rounds around the blanket with:
Ch 2, 3 dtr in the next ch loop; rep * to *
and end with ch 2. In the corners work 3
dtr in the ch loop, ch 3, 3 dtr in the same
loop. Work 1 rnd around the entire blanket
with 5 dtr in each ch loop and 10 dtr in each
corner. Cut yarn, weave in ends on WS, and
gently steam press blanket.

Kitchen Towel

A flower border on a kitchen towel—maybe that seems like too much work for something to be used only for drying, but, of course, you can also make these towels for show or knit several and use them as napkins!

MATERIALS

Yarn: Dale of Norway Lerke
1 ball Yellow 2215
4 balls White 0020

Crochet hook: U.K. size 11 / 3 mm
Needles: 12 in / 33 cm long straight or short circular U.K. size 11 / 3 mm

This towel has 7 flowers across the width on one side and is 34 in / 86 cm long, including the flower border.

Follow the instructions for the Place Mat (page 59) but use yellow for the first 2 rnds of the flowers and white for the rest of the flower and knitted towel.

Primroses are used for the edging of place mats and kitchen towels.

For our outdoor summer table, we crocheted the edges of the place mats and matching kitchen towels with primroses. You can also use the kitchen towels as napkins.

Summer

Primrose Throw

Here's another variation on the throw inspired by our primroses. We crocheted masses of little flowers and then crocheted them together for a large throw. The only "rule" was that the same two colors never meet. This is a project for anyone with plenty of patience and time.

MATERIALS
Crochet hook: U.K. size 9 / 3.5 mm and leftover yarn suitable for hook size

Whole Flower
Rnd 1: Ch 6 and join into a ring with 1 sl st into 1st ch.
Rnd 2: Ch 5 (= 1 dtr and 1 ch), (1 dtr around ring, ch 1) around until there are total of 12 dtr and 12 ch. End with 1 sl st into 1st dtr (= 4th ch at beg).

Rnd 3: Change color and ch 4 (= 1 dtr), 1 dtr around ch loop, (ch 2, 2 dtr in next ch loop) around and end with 1 st st into top of beg ch.

Rnd 4: Change color. Turn work, (2 dc around ch loop, ch 3, 2 dc around same ch loop) in each ch loop around. End with 1 sl st into 1st dc; cut yarn and bring end through rem st.

For rest of the flowers, crochet the flower

dtr), 1 dtr around ch loop, ch 2 (2 dtr in next ch loop, ch 2) around and end with 2 dtr into last ch loop.

Rnd 4: Crochet as for the whole flower when the flower is joined with another.

This throw has 21 whole and 2 half flowers across the width and is 25 whole and 2 half flowers in length. We used a total of 11 half flowers as an edging on the short side and 26 half flowers on the long side.

We edged the throw with 4 dtr in the center of every half flower and 4 dtr around the outer dtr of the half flowers. We rounded the corners with 10 dtr.

to another one on the 4th rnd.

Joining

Crochet with the yarn for flower number 2. Work *2 dc around a ch loop of flower #2, ch 1 and 2 dc around a ch loop of flower #1. Ch 1, 2 dc around the same ch loop on flower #2*; rep * to * 2 times to join the flowers.

Two flowers meet only in two ch loops and are crocheted together with 2 "mouse teeth."

Half Flowers for the Edging

Rnd 1: Ch 6 and join into a ring with 1 sl st into 1st ch.

Rnd 2: Ch 5 (= 1 dtr and 1 ch), (1 dtr around ring, ch 1) around 6 times and end with 1 dtr.

Rnd 3: Turn and change color. Ch 4 (= 1

Embroidered Pillows for the Garden, Four Pansy Variations

Embroider pillows inspired by the wild flowers in the garden and use them outside when the weather permits. Here we've decorated an old bench at the end of the garden with 4 pillows. That still leaves a place for us to sit or lie down and mediate on nice summer days.

The pillows are embroidered with diamond stitch. We used Dale of Norway Hubro yarn so the work goes quickly. We didn't think the yellow on the Hubro color card was strong enough, so substituted Dale of Norway Freestyle instead. The canvas is called "Maxi Canvas" (item #387) from Permin. The finished embroidery is 21¼ in / 54 cm wide and 20¾ in / 52.5 cm long.

Diamond Stitch

| Begin with a diagonal stitch from left to right. | Make a diagonal stitch back from right to left. | The third stitch is at the center from the bottom up. | The last stitch is crossways over from left to right. |

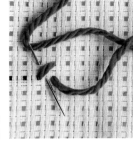
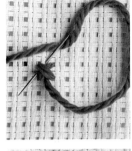

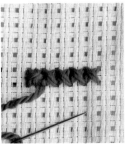

When making many stitches with the same color, you can kill two birds with one stone, working the first cross at top speed. The last stitch should always go the same way, whether you choose to make it horizontal or vertical at the end.

Carlos is sewing the lining for the pillows out on the veranda, which also serves as a sewing room during the summer months.

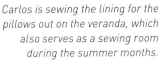

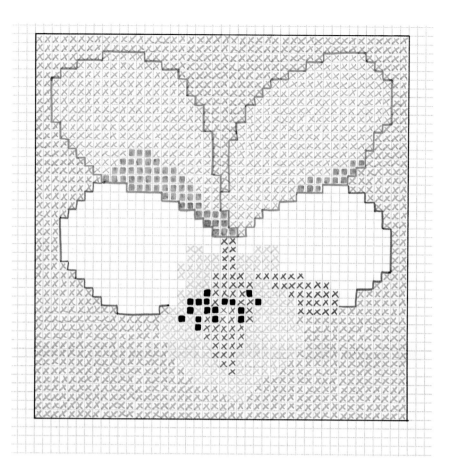

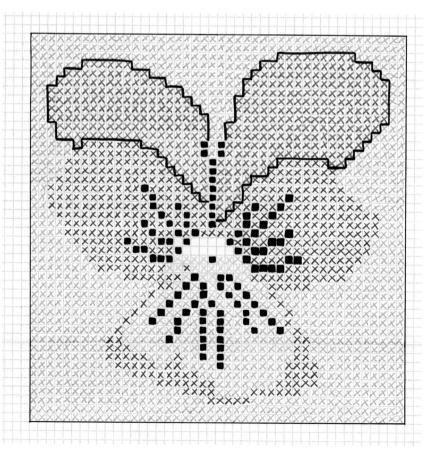

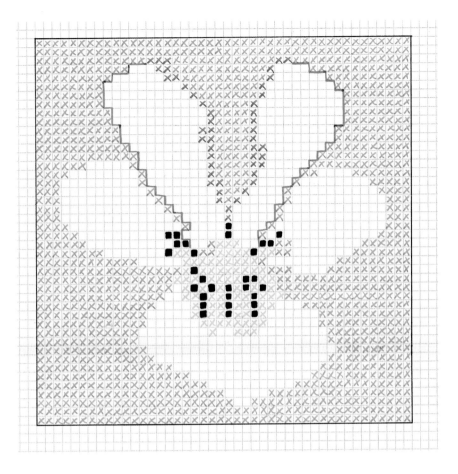

Pillow No. 1

Pillow No. 2

MATERIALS
Yarn: Dale of Norway Hubro
Beige 2631
White 0020
Light Pink 3810
Old Rose 4132
Dark Beige 2643
Red-violet 4526
Black 0090
Dale of Norway Freestyle:
doubled strand of Yellow 2106

MATERIALS
Yarn: Dale of Norway Hubro
Beige 2631
Light Purple 4132
Dark Blue 5764
Light Blue 6622
Black 0090
White 0020
Dale of Norway Freestyle: doubled
strand of Yellow 2106

Pillow Backing
Cut 2 pieces of fabric (Basque linen, for example).
The first piece is the top part of the back and measures 22¾ x 18½ in / 58 cm x 47 cm = ¾ in / 2 cm seam allowance on each side, ¾ in / 2 cm seam allowance at the top and 2 in / 5 cm facing on the wrong side for the pillow opening.

Fold the facing down (2 in / 5 cm long) and sew down.

The second piece of fabric is the lower part of the backing and measures 22¾ x 9½ in / 58 cm x 24.5 cm = ¾ in / 2 cm seam allowance on each side, ¾ in / 2 cm seam allowance at lower edge of pillow and 2 in / 5 cm under the facing of the top part + 2 in / 5 cm facing. Seam the lower edge.

MATERIALS

Yarn: Dale of Norway Hubro
Beige 2631
White 0020
Purple 5036
Black 0090
Dale of Norway Freestyle:
doubled strand of Yellow 2106

MATERIALS

Yarn: Dale of Norway Hubro
Beige 2631
White 0020
Light Purple 4132
Purple 5036
Red 4227
Black 0090
Dale of Norway Freestyle: doubled
strand of Yellow 2106

Sew buttonholes in the top fold of the top section. For example, 3 buttonholes, and then sew 3 buttons on the lower section.

Place the two pieces of fabric against one another, with the smallest piece/ lower part, below the larger piece/top part, with exactly 2 in / 5 cm overlap. Pin them together and pin the fabric to the embroidery with RS facing RS and sew

all around the pillow. Cut off the excess canvas and zigzag or overlock around the edges. Steam press the seam open and turn the pillow cover right side out.

A pillow insert 24 x 24 in / 60 x 60 cm should fit perfectly.

A little secret: We actually used snaps; 3 large black ones.

Embroidered Table Mats

Here is Pillow no. 2 embroidered with cross stitch in a different color scheme on finer canvas. It's large enough to also serve as a table mat.

MATERIALS
Canvas: Aida 4.4 from Permin.
Yarn: Dale of Norway Daletta
Light Blue 5703
Purple 5052
Red 4255
Pink 4711
Black 0090
Yellow 2015
White 0010
See pages 72-73 for charts.

Pansies embroidered for a wall hanging in the dollhouse in the garden.

Embroider

A FLOWER THROW

Our garden is composed the same way as we crochet throws, no plan, just a lot of colors. The plants are moved when we see they aren't doing well where they are, not because the colors are "wrong." Nothing is wrong here. We try to group plants that bloom at different times, so we'll have flowers from early spring until the first snowfall. In the weeks before the perennials start blooming, we arrange big pots of summer flowers in the flower beds.

Often our garden is very pretty when the first snow comes and some of the flowers continue to bloom. Orange California poppies coated with snow are beautiful, as are frosted blue asters.

Flower Meadow

The mice and the hippies are enjoying a cozy picnic
in the flower meadow.

It is lucky that Hippie brought her own
crocheted blanket with her. In the flower
meadow one can lie on a bed of flowers and
rest between work sessions.

Magnus Garden Mouse has worked hard
all day. It is so nice that there is a flower
meadow in the garden where he can take
a well-earned rest today!

It is so nice here! Hippie is happy to
take off her pretty shoes decorated
with primroses so she can run bare-
foot in a sea of flowers.

You'll find the flower meadow a little bit away, at the south side of the garden. We let the wild flowers grow free here and cut the grass only once or twice each summer. We don't cut the entire area, just a little strip for a walkway. Our idea is that the flowers will re-seed themselves where we haven't taken the grass out. It makes a little meadow, a delightful lap rug of flowers.

Mmmm, we've made a good spread with all the tasty fruits from the garden: raspberries, blueberries, strawberries, and cherries, to go with some coffee and tea.

The garden grows as randomly as a lap rug. Sometimes it is so full of plants in one bed that we have to make a new bed wherever we can find room. This encapsulates our philosophy both in the garden and our handwork!

Throw Knit with All Sorts of Leftover Yarns and Colors

These leftover yarn throws are perfect if you are looking for a simple pattern and an effective way to use up a lot of yarn. They are also easy to knit. The secret behind these throws is also simple: work as randomly as possible for the best results.

MATERIALS

Leftover yarns
Needles: 32 in / 80 cm circular U.K. size 9–10 / 3.5 mm.

INSTRUCTIONS

CO 250 sts. Working back and forth, knit 2 rows with one color. Change colors and knit another two rows. Keep changing colors the same way until the piece is approx 71 in / 180 cm long, a good length. If you run out of a color mid-row, just change to a new color.

Be careful not to "lock in" the edge stitches: Check to make sure the yarn is placed correctly when you begin a new row. The yarn you are knitting with must come behind the work, between the 1st and 2nd sts. The first st is always slipped purlwise. If you consistently change the colors this way, your throw will have a nice edge on each side, with stitches lying smoothly over each other. After a few rows, changing colors correctly will come automatically.

Scarecrow

Hippie has a summer job as a scarecrow. No one would say that Hippie is overly demanding. Spending the summer on a stick in the kitchen garden is quite fine. It's not bad working for food. She is not completely scary because we don't want to frighten the life out of dogs, cats, birds, or little animals. We only want to scare them a little, just enough to keep them away from the tomatoes and other plants.

Hat and Shabby Scarecrow Sweater

Hippie dressed up as a scarecrow with a sweater of leftover yarns knitted as for the Garden Mouse, only with some extra rounds on the body. Don't weave in the ends so the sweater will look properly shabby.

Hat

MATERIALS

Yarn: The hat is knitted with leftover yarns suitable for the recommended needles.

Needles: Set of 5 dpn U.K. 11 / 3 mm
Crochet hook: U.K. size 11 / 3 mm

INSTRUCTIONS

CO 12 sts and divide over 4 dpn, with 3 sts on each needle.

Rnd 1: K12.
Rnd 2: (K1, inc 1, k1, inc 1, k1) around.
Rnd 3: K20.
Rnd 4: (K1, inc 1, k3, inc 1, k1) around.
Rnd 5: K28.
Rnd 6: (K1, inc 1, k5, inc 1, k1) around – 36 sts.
Rnds 7 – 26: Knit.
Rnd 27: (Inc 1, k1) around.
Rnds 28 – 37: Knit (or work to desired brim length).
Rnd 38: Work eyelets: (K2tog, yo) around.
Rnd 39: Knit.

BO knitwise. Work 3 tr in each hole of the eyelet round. Begin with 1 dc, ch 3 (= 1 tr). End with 1 sl st to top of beg ch. Weave in ends and gently steam press hat.

Guerrilla Knitting

All hippies seem to have a message and it usually has to do with love and peace. Our hippies also think the world could be a little more pleasant, so they've started guerrilla knitting. They decorate everything that comes in their path. They believe that handwork is beautiful and it's not crazy to embellish the things we use in everyday life as long as it is handmade. Yes, the message is totally simple: The future is handmade!

The stakes for the plant supports and hand tools are knitted with leftover yarns and 3 dpn. We used needles U.K. size 11 / 3 mm. When it comes to plant supports, we cast on 8 sts, divided them onto 2 ndls, joined, and worked around to the desired length with a third needle. For the hand tools, we cast on as many stitches as needed for the circumference of the handle. Swatch to see what will fit your tools.

Yes, to
the future

Granny Squares

You can never have enough cozy blankets for cool summer evenings. We make some every time we clear out the yarns in the storage room. We use what we have.

A few rounds of treble crochet groups as an edging around the throw are nice. We don't sew or crochet the squares together as is usually done. We used to do that but it looked a little sloppy, particularly after so many hours and days of crocheting. We'll explain our way of joining so you can try it yourself.

Some of the rounds are worked with a two or more strands of yarn held together. When using leftover yarns, experiment to see what works. Holding several strands together works well because if it is too thick or too thin, you simply have to remove or add a strand as necessary. You can save the extras for another project with different size hook.

A throw 8 squares wide and 10 squares long is a good size. A throw that size will weigh about 4½ pounds / 2 kilos, and use about 4 balls of yarn for joining. Of course, this should be taken with a grain of salt: since you'll be working with the yarn you like, the size can vary quite a bit.

If you don't have any yarn on hand or the dyelots for the joining aren't the same, you may need to buy some yarn. Don't worry,

we won't send the yarn police after you. This is, after all, just a remnants throw.

When it comes to leftover yarn blankets, we don't have any inhibitions. We break all the rules and have so much fun that it's difficult to stop. Should you need a tepee, two large blankets are enough to make one.

MATERIALS
Crochet hook: U.K. size 9 / 3.5 mm and yarn for recommended hook size

INSTRUCTIONS
Work Rnds 1 and 2 with the same color or change color on every round.

> **Tip 1:** When you change color, you can begin the next round where you like. It is usually best, though, to begin at a corner and, with each color change, to rotate the corner you begin on so that the square is as even as possible.
>
> **Tip 2:** When you change color, hold the old color so that you can catch and cover it as you work and avoid weaving in ends later on.

Rnd 1: Ch 8 and join into a ring with 1 sl st to 1st ch.

Rnd 2: Ch 4 (=1 dtr), 3 dtr around ring, (ch 3, 4 dtr around ring) 3 times, ch 3 and end with 1 sl st to top of beg ch.

Rnd 5: 16 dtr groups.

Rnd 6: 20 dtr groups.

Rnd 3: Ch 4 (=1 dtr), 3 dtr around ch loop, ch 3, 4 dtr around same loop, (ch 2, 4 dtr around next ch loop, ch 3, 4 dtr around same loop) 3 times, ch 2 and end with 1 sl st to top of beg ch.

Now you have 8 dtr groups with 4 dtr in each ch loop in between.

The ch-3 loops form the corners.

Continuing crocheting with 4 dtr in each ch-2 loops and 4 dtr, ch 3, 4 dtr in each corner. There should be 2 ch between each dtr group along the sides.

Rnd 4: 12 dtr groups.

Rnd 7: 24 dtr groups.

How to Make Crochet a Little Less Boring—Trick No. 1

Sometimes crochet can be rather boring, especially if the blanket is very big. We gather all our colors into a basket, pull out Color 1 and work Rnds 1 and 2 with it. We put that ball of yarn on the table and pull out Color 2 for Rnd 3 and put that yarn beside the first. We continue taking yarn from the basket until we have 6 balls on the table and the first square is complete. If we pull a yarn from the basket that is already on the table, we try another. For the second square, we put the first ball away and add a new one to the back of the line. That way, the second color for the first square becomes the first color of the second square.

Since we use a lot of leftover yarns, sometimes there are a few very small balls of yarn. In that case, we use the smallest ball for Rnds 1 and 2 and let it change place with a larger ball.

Before too long, the crochet almost goes by itself and the excitement lies in which ball of yarn will be the next color. This way, there is little chance that you'll have two squares alike. It's also fun to let children pick out some yarns to chain together. Ask them to find two alike so they'll have something to keep them occupied.

How to Make Crochet a Little Less Boring—Trick No. 2

Get a ball of yarn and work Rnds 1 and 2 of a square, take a second ball and work Rnd 3 of the first square and then Rnds 1 and 2 of a new square. With a third ball, work Rnd 4 of the 1st square, Rnd 3 of square 2, and Rnds 1 and 2 of a new square. Continue the same way until you have 7 rnds on each of the squares. If you draw small balls out of the basket, the system can get out of balance and suddenly you have a lot of squares underway. Before you know it, you have enough squares for several blankets.

Joining the Squares

You can join the squares one by one until the strip is desired width. Begin with an edging on the first square of strip.

Begin in one corner and work 1 dc into ch loop, ch 3, 1 dc in the same loop, *1 dc between the 1st and 2nd dtr of a dtr-group, 1 dc, ch 3, 1 dc between the 2nd and 3rd dtr of a dtr-group, 1 dc between the 3rd and 4th dtr of a dtr-group; 1 dc I ch loop, ch 3, 1 dc in the same chain*; rep * to * to corner; 1 dc in ch loop, ch 1.

the second square. *1 dc between the 1st and 2nd dtr of the dtr-group on the second square, 1 dc, ch 1, 1 dc in the next ch loop of the first square, ch 1, 1 dc back between the 2nd and 3rd dtr of the dtr-group of the second square, 1 dc between the 3rd and 4th dtr of dtr-group, 1 dc in ch loop on the second square, ch 1, 1 dc in the next ch loop of the first square, ch 1, 1 dc in the same ch loop on the second square*; rep* to * to the corner. Cut yarn and pull end through last st.

Now you can crochet the first square to the second or join two strips without cutting the yarn.

Begin at the corner of the second square and work 1 tr in ch loop, ch 1, 1 dc in same loop. Work 1 tr in the dc at the corner of the first square and then 1 dc in the ch loop you just crocheted into on

Now you can join the strips one by one to desired length. The strips are joined as for the squares, but, in the space between squares, work 1 dc in the dtr on one strip, ch 3, and 1 dc in the dtr on the second strip.

When joining borders, crochet them together the same way, with 1 dc in the first point marked with a red thread (see photo), ch 3, 1 dc in the second point marked with red thread. When crocheting back, there will be 1 dc at the second point, ch 1, 1 dc in the loop, ch 1 and 1 dc back in the first point marked with red thread.

PERENNIALS

Every year we are always amazed. In May there is almost nothing in the ground, except maybe some dried out remains of the previous year's perennials, and suddenly, like magic, after a few weeks of light, heat, and rain, there they are—Columbines, iris, poppies, malva, anemone, and the garden's blue flowers, with Meconopsis as a blue queen! We welcome the perennials year after year!

Garter Stitch

MATERIALS

Needles: straight U.K. size 11 / 3 mm and Light DK yarn

INSTRUCTIONS

All of the bands are worked on 2 needles back and forth over 10 sts. The length is determined by the number of ridges. 1 ridge = 2 knit rows, worked back and forth. Leave a long tail when you finish knitting and you can use it for joining the bands. The ends of the bands are sewn together into a ring before the long sides are folded down. This way, different bands can lie inside each other to form shapes.

Bands have 8, 18, 28, 38, 50, or 70 ridges. When counting ridges, hold the piece towards you with the cast-on tail on the right side. When you bind off, the tail should end up on the left side of the piece.

Joining the Bands

Lay the bands inside each other, shaping as shown, and, using the yarn tails, sew them together through the edge sts on the wrong/ under side of the piece. End on the right side, sewing and shaping the piece using thread the same color as for the outermost band. Check the right side and then weave in the ends on the underside so the pieces don't shift and lose their shape.

Pin Cushion

We saw this method of joining knitted bands many years ago on a simple pin cushion composed of 5 rings. Our pin cushion has become a flower with 7 circles.

MATERIALS

Yarn: Dale of Norway Falk, 1 ball of each color:
Dark Purple 5036
Light Purple 5144
Yellow 2417

Needles: U.K. size 11 / 3 mm

INSTRUCTIONS

Knit 6 light purple bands with 8 ridges each.
Knit 6 dark purple bands with 18 ridges each.
Knit 1 yellow band with 8 ridges.
Knit 1 yellow band with 18 ridges.

See page 98 for general instructions and joining.

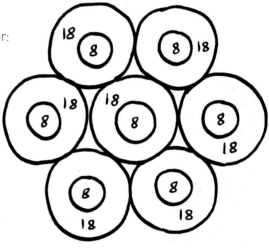

Seat Cushion, Inspired by Blue Poppies

The flowers are composed of bands with 8 and 18 ridges. The flower's eye is a yellow ring surrounded by six blue rings for the flower petals. Each ring has a 70-ridge band around it. Between the flowers are rings with 8, 18, and 28 ridges. Sew the flowers together securely with brown yarn.

MATERIALS

Yarn: Dale of Norway Falk in shades of blue:
1 ball Blue 5563
1 ball Blue 5813
1 ball Blue 6027
1 ball Yellow 2417
5 balls Brown 3070

Needles: U.K. size 11 / 3 mm

INSTRUCTIONS

9 yellow bands with 8 ridges each.
9 yellow bands with 18 ridges each.
12 blue 5563 bands with 18 ridges each.
12 blue 5563 bands with 18 ridges each.
18 blue 5813 bands with 8 ridges each.
18 blue 5813 bands with 18 ridges each.
18 blue 5822 bands with 8 ridges each.
18 blue 5822 bands with 18 ridges each.
6 blue 6027 bands with 8 ridges each.
6 blue 6027 bands with 18 ridges each.
4 brown bands with 8 ridges each.
4 brown bands with 18 ridges each.
4 brown bands with 28 ridges each.
9 brown bands with 70 ridges each.

See page 98 for general instructions and joining.

Knitted Bags

These bags have so many different uses, from saving seeds and jewelry to fragrant bags filled with potpourri or lavender.

MATERIALS

Yarn: Dale of Norway Vipe, one ball of each color

Needles: Set of 5 dpn U.K. size 13 / 2.5 mm
Crochet hook: U.K. size 12 / 2.5 mm

INSTRUCTIONS

With dpn, CO 12 sts, divide onto 4 dpn (3 sts on each needle), and join. The sts on each needle are used for 1 repeat of the charted pattern. The cast-on is represented by the bottom row of 3 sts on the chart.

Rnd 1: Knit.
Rnd 2: (K2, inc 1, k1) around.
Rnd 3: Knit around – 16 sts.
Rnd 4: (K1, inc 1, k2, inc 1, k1) around.
Rnd 5: Knit around – 24 sts.
Rnd 6: (K1, inc 1, k4, inc 1, k1) around.
Rnd 7: Knit around – 32 sts.
Rnd 8: (K1, inc 1, k6, inc 1, k1) around.
Rnd 9: Knit around – 40 sts.
Rnd 10: (K1, inc 1, k8, inc 1, k1) around.
Rnd 11: Knit around – 48 sts.
Rnd 12: (K1, inc 1, k10, inc 1, k1) around.
Rnd 13: Knit around – 56 sts.
Rnd 14: (K1, inc 1, k12, inc 1, k1) around.

Rnd 15: Knit around – 64 sts.
Rnd 16: (K1, inc 1, k14, inc 1, k1) around.
Rnd 17: Knit around – 72 sts.
Rnd 18: (K1, inc 1, k16, inc 1, k1) around.
Rnds 19 – 41: Knit around – 80 sts.
Rnd 42: (K1, k2tog, k17) around.
Rnd 43: Knit around – 76 sts.
Rnd 44: (K1, k2tog, k13, k2tog, k1) around.
Rnd 45: Knit around – 68 sts.
Rnd 46: (K1, k2tog, k11, k2tog, k1) around.
Rnd 47: Knit around – 60 sts.
Rnd 48: (K1, k2tog, k9, k2tog, k1) around – 52 sts rem.
Rnd 49: (K6, k2tog, k5) around – 48 sts.
Rnd 50: (K1, k2tog, k6, k2tog, k1) around – 40 sts rem.
Rnd 51: (K2tog, yo) around.
Rnd 52: Knit around.
Rnd 53: BO knitwise.

Crochet an edging around the top of the bag working into the holes of the eyelet round: (1 dc, ch 2, 2 tr, ch 2, 1 dc) in each eyelet.
Crochet a cord: ch 80 or thread a silk ribbon through the eyelets.

Jewelry Bag

Wrap your finest jewels in silk paper and keep them in a knitted bag. This one is embellished with blue birds and vintage ribbon with yellow flowers threaded through the eyelets on the bag. The bird is from a Peruvian pattern.

MATERIALS

Yarn: Dale of Norway Vipe, one ball of each color:
White 0020
Blue 5852

Needles: Set of 5 dpn U.K. size 13 / 2.5 mm
Crochet hook: U.K. size 12 / 2.5 mm

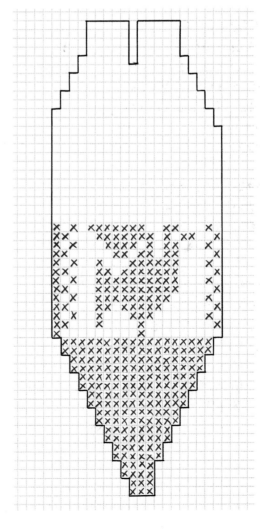

Seed Bag

Gather all the seed packets and loose seeds from the garden in a knitted bag embellished with violets. Put the garden seeds in small plastic or paper bags first.

MATERIALS

Yarn: Dale of Norway Vipe, one ball of each color:
White 0020
Green 7224
Purple 5024

Needles: Set of 5 dpn U.K. size 13 / 2.5 mm
Crochet hook: U.K. size 12 / 2.5 mm

See page 106 for basic instructions.

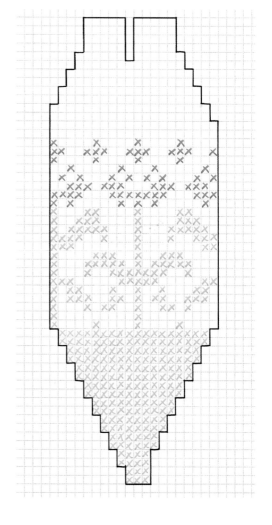

Potpourri Bag

Fill a bag with dried rose petals, lavender, and other fragrant leaves and flowers and leave it in the dresser or chest with the bedding. You can also use this in the bath.

MATERIALS

Yarn: Dale of Norway Vipe, one ball of each color:
White 0020
Green 7224
Orange 3607

Needles: Set of 5 dpn U.K. size 13 / 2.5 mm
Crochet hook: U.K. size 12 / 2.5 mm

See page 106 for basic instructions.

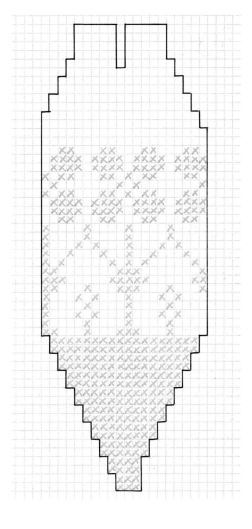

You can find butterflies in every possible color combination so use your imagination to make your own unique butterfly.

Butterfly 1

Name: Vanessa Atalanta

MATERIALS

Yarn: Dale of Norway Heilo
2 balls Black 0090
2 balls Brown 2642
1 ball Red 4018
1 ball Bright White 0010

Needles: U.K. size 11 / 3 mm

INSTRUCTIONS

2 red bands with 38 ridges each.
2 red bands with 50 ridges each.
8 white bands with 8 ridges each.
6 black bands with 8 ridges each.
2 black bands with 70 ridges each.
2 black bands with 28 ridges each.
1 brown band with 70 ridges each.
2 brown bands with 8 ridges each.
4 brown bands with 18 ridges each.
2 brown bands with 28 ridges each.
2 brown bands with 50 ridges each.

See page 98 for general instructions and joining.

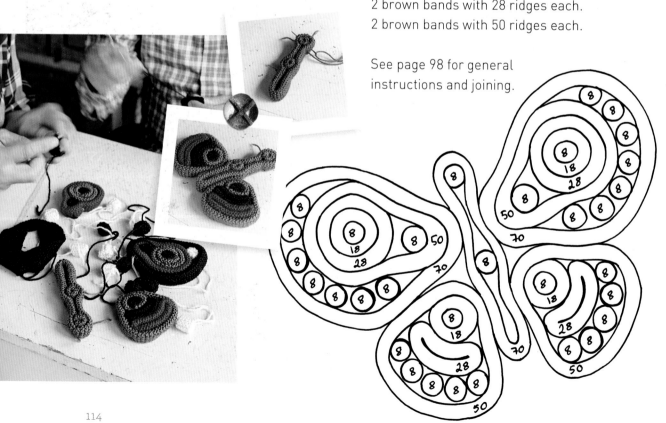

114

Butterfly 2

Name: Lysandra Bellargus

MATERIALS

Yarn: Dale of Norway Heilo
3 balls Light blue 5813
1 ball Dark blue 5744
1 ball White 0020

Needles: U.K. size 11 / 3 mm

INSTRUCTIONS

14 dark blue bands with 8 ridges each.
1 dark blue band with 70 ridges each.
2 light blue bands with 8 ridges each.
4 light blue bands with 18 ridges each.
4 light blue bands with 28 ridges each.
4 light blue bands with 50 ridges each.
2 light blue bands with 70 ridges each.
6 white bands with 8 ridges each.

See page 98 for general instructions
and joining.

Butterfly 3

A butterfly inspired by drawings in the book *Botanicals* by Assouline.

MATERIALS

Yarn: Dale of Norway Heilo, 1 ball of each color:
Black 0083
Gray 0007
Light gray 0004
Yellow 2126
Red 4018
Blue 5943

Needles: U.K. size 11 / 3 mm

INSTRUCTIONS

2 black bands with 70 ridges each.
10 black bands with 18 ridges each.
4 yellow bands with 50 ridges each.
1 light gray band with 70 ridges each.
2 light gray bands with 8 ridges each.
2 gray bands with 18 ridges each.
2 gray bands with 50 ridges each.
2 blue bands with 8 ridges each.
6 red bands with 8 ridges each.

See page 98 for general instructions and joining.

DAISIES

Hippie crochets daisies in all sorts of colors. The leftover yarn basket is almost empty and she knows that she should use up her yarn stash and put a little order in her life. She *needs* to do that, but then who doesn't? Crocheted squares will make a blanket as colorful as Hippie's garden and as colorful as she wants the rest of the world to be.

Coasters for Glasses and Mugs

MATERIALS

Yarn: Dale of Norway Falk and Freestyle
100 g is enough for 5 flowers.
We used white, red, pink, blue, yellow and
other colors

Crochet hook: U.K. size 9 / 3.5 mm

INSTRUCTIONS

Rnd 1: Ch 8 and join into a ring with 1 sl st
into 1st ch.

Rnd 2: Ch 6 (= 1 dtr + ch 2), (1 dtr around

Rnd 4: Turn and work 1 dc in 1st ch loop,
*ch 14, 1 dc in the same loop, ch 2, 1 dc
in the next ch loop. Turn and ch 3, 15 dtr

around the 14-ch loop. Ch 3
and work 1 dc in the top of
the 1st dtr where the petal
is attached*. Rep * to * a total of 12
times, ending with 1 dc in the ch loop
where the 1st petal was worked.

Weave in ends on WS and gently
steam press. Shape the petals so
they are slightly
angled. Pull the
double trebles
into place so
they sit evenly on
the chain loops.

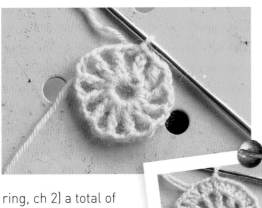

ring, ch 2) a total of
12 times. End with
1 sl st into 4th ch at
beg of rnd.

Rnd 3: Ch 3 (= 1 tr), 2
tr in 1st ch loop, ch 1,
(3 tr in next ch loop, ch 1) around and end
with 1 sl st to top of ch 3.

Chair Cushion

MATERIALS

Yarn: Dale of Norway Freestyle
Flower center: 1 ball yellow 2106
Petals:
2 balls White 0020
2 balls Green 8045
1 ball Black 0090

Crochet hook: U.K. size 9 / 3.5 mm. We used a smaller hook than usual for this yarn so the cushion would be firmer than if worked with a larger hook.

INSTUCTIONS

Flower

Rnd 1: Ch 8 and join into a ring with 1 sl st into 1st ch.

Rnd 2: Ch 6 (= 1 dtr + ch 2), (1 dtr around ring, ch 2) a total of 12 times. End with 1 sl st into 4th ch at beg of rnd.

Rnd 3: Ch 3 (= 1 dtr), 2 dtr in 1st ch loop, ch 1, (3 dtr in next ch loop, ch 1) around and end with 1 sl st to top of beg ch.

Rnd 4: Turn and work 1 dc in 1st ch loop, *ch 14, 1 dc in the same loop, ch 2, 1 dc in the next ch loop. Turn and ch 3, 15 dtr around the 14-ch loop. Ch 3 and work 1 dc in the top of the 1st dtr where the petal is attached*. Rep * to * a total of 12 times, ending with 1 dc in the ch loop where the 1st petal was worked.

Background

The background begins at the tr groups around the chain loops behind the flower petals (see photos here and on page 128).

Rnd 1: Ch 4 (= 1 dtr), 2 dtr in ch loop, ch 3 and 3 dtr in the same ch loop, *(ch 2, 3 dtr in the next ch loop) 2 times, ch 2, 3 dtr in the next ch loop, ch 3, 3 dtr in the same ch loop (= corner)*; rep * to * a total of 3 times, work (ch 2, 3 dtr in the next ch loop) 2 times, ch 2 and end with 1 sl st into top of ch at beg.

Rnd 2: Turn and crochet back. Begin the first dtr group with ch 4. Continue as for Rnd 1, with one more 3-dtr group along each side between corners).

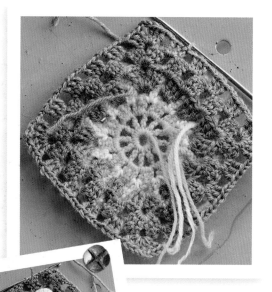

Beginning at the corner of the second square, work 1 tr in the ch loop, ch 1 and 1 dc in the same loop. Work 1 tr in the dc at the corner of the first square and then 1 dc in the ch loop you just worked into on the second square. *1 dc between the 1st and 2nd dtr of the dtr group of the second square, ch 1, 1 dc in the next ch loop of the first square, ch 1, 1 dc between the 2nd and 3rd dtr of the dtr group on the second square, 1 dc in the ch loop of the second square, ch 1, 1 dc in the next ch loop of the first square, ch 1, 1 dc in the same loop of the second square*; rep * to * to the corner.

Cut yarn and pull end through last st.

Join the strips one by one as for joining the squares until the piece is desired length, but, in the space between the squares, work 1 dc in the dtr of one strip, ch 3, and 1 dc in the dtr of the second strip.

Rnd 3: Turn and work back. Begin the first dtr group with ch 4. Continue as for Rnd 1, with one more 3-dtr group along each side between corners.

Joining the Squares

See the explanation and photos on page 92.

Join the squares one by one, beginning with an edge on the first square or strip, until the cushion is desired width.

Attach yarn to one corner and work 1 dc in the ch loop, ch 3, 1 dc in the same loop, *1 dc between the 1st and 2nd dtr of the dtr group, ch 3, 1 dc between the 2nd and 3rd dtr of the dtr group, 1 dc in the ch loop, ch 3, 1 dc in the same loop*; rep * to * to the corner, 1 dc in ch loop, ch 1. Now crochet the first square together with the second square or strip without cutting the yarn.

We've drawn a lot of inspiration from daisies and chrysanthemums.

Chrysanthemum

MATERIALS

Yarn: Dale of Norway Heilo, 1 ball of each color:
Yellow 2136
Light pink 4203
Dark pink 4624

Needles: U.K. size 11 / 3 mm

INSTRUCTIONS

1 yellow band with 8 ridges.
1 yellow band with 18 ridges.
8 light pink bands with 38 ridges each.
8 dark pink bands with 38 ridges each.

This table mat, shaped like a chrysanthemum, is made as for the flowers. See page 98 for general instructions and joining.

WIND CHIMES

No garden is complete without relaxing sounds. Here's a little idea for making use of scrap metal you have on hand because everyone has things they never manage to throw out. Maybe your chime is a kitchen spoon hitting a fork or a metal pipe against a key.

We use junk for a wind chime in the garden, a chime of junk. You'll need some various types of metal that will make sounds, a drill, metal rings or nylon cord, and a metal bore. We used metal rings for a clink every now and then but nylon cord will make them clink more.

This chime is made with an old light fixture.

We have a wind chime from Japan that was clanging all the time so we hung a thick piece of crystal in the center and now we hear the chimes only intermittently. Now it is pleasant because it can be a little too much as it is very windy where we live.

Decorations from a flower pot made suitable hangings for this wind chime.

CONCLUSION

Some plants live their own lives: Forsythia bushes that had yellow flowers in May now have large white bells. It is the white bell that has taken root in the bush and stretches out to the sun. That's absolutely okay, as it should be, as long as it wants.

Now it's time to note what needs to be moved next spring—which plants became too tightly packed this summer. Seeds can sprout in the pots as soon as they are ready. If they go to seed, we'll have something to share with friends. Hortensias and roses in pots have to be brought in because they need to rest until next Easter, when they'll get water and light and we will have beautiful flowers. Nothing is cut down until next year so all the nourishment goes back into the plant and soil.

One last round of weeding has to be done, a last stand against the gout weed: We pick the leaves and hope that it will die out one fine day. It smells good; it smells like fall.

After that, we just have to give it up for the winter, cover the plants that need covering, and brought inside. So, we can only wait for spring, dream and make plans for next year while we crochet, knit, embroider, and stay cozy during the dark winter evenings. We always bring in a little of the summer during the coldest time of the year. And it is true to say that the summer is long, and it is good to be able to stay in and just be for a few months.

Thank you and we wish you a good summer!